THE OFFICIAL CELTIC
ANNUAL 2017

CONTENTS

CLUB HONOURS

SCOTTISH LEAGUE WINNERS [47 TIMES]

892/93, 1893/94, 1895/96, 1897/98,
904/05, 1905/06, 1906/07, 1907/08,
908/09, 1909/10, 1913/14, 1914/15,
915/16, 1916/17, 1918/19, 1921/22,
925/26, 1935/36, 1937/38, 1953/54,
965/66, 1966/67, 1967/68, 1968/69,
969/70, 1970/71, 1971/72, 1972/73,
973/74, 1976/77, 1978/79, 1980/81,
981/82, 1985/86, 1987/88, 1997/98,
2000/01, 2001/02, 2003/04, 2005/06,
2006/07, 2007/08, 2011/12, 2012/13,
2013/14, 2014/15, 2015/16

SCOTTISH CUP WINNERS [36 TIMES]

892, 1899, 1900, 1904, 1907, 1908,
911, 1912, 1914, 1923, 1925, 1927,
931, 1933, 1937, 1951, 1954, 1965,
967, 1969, 1971, 1972, 1974, 1975,
977, 1980, 1985, 1988, 1989, 1995,
2001, 2004, 2005, 2007, 2011, 2013

LEAGUE CUP WINNERS [15 TIMES]

956/57, 1957/58, 1965/66, 1966/67,
967/68, 1968/69, 1969/70, 1974/75,
982/83, 1997/98, 1999/00, 2000/01,
2005/06, 2008/09, 2014/15

EUROPEAN CUP WINNERS 1967

CORONATION CUP WINNERS 1953

BRENDAN RODGERS

MANAGER FACTFILE:

D.O.B: 26/01/73

BORN: CARNLOUGH, IRELAND

PLAYING CAREER RECORD:
BALLYMENA UNITED (1987-90)
READING (1990-93)
NEWPORT (1993-94)
WITNEY TOWN (1994-95)
NEWBURY TOWN (1995-96)

MANAGER RECORD:
WATFORD (2008-09)
READING (2009)
SWANSEA CITY (2010-12)
LIVERPOOL (2012-15)

BRENDAN Rodgers has been steeped in the Celtic tradition all of his life. On May 20, 2016 his dream came true when the Irishman was made manager of Celtic Football Club and he took a bow as over 13,000 supporters turned out to welcome him to the club on that Monday afternoon.

Celtic were a long way off, though, when the youngster from Carnlough started playing youth football with Ballymena United in 1984, before he was even in his teens, and three years later when he joined the club on a more professional basis.

He was still in his teens when Brendan caught the eye of scouts from across the water and was on his way to join Reading as an 18-year-old. Unfortunately, by the time he was 20, a knee condition had forced him to retire from the playing side at professional level but Brendan continued to play the game at non-league level while taking up coaching further up the ladder.

Brendan remained as a coach at Reading and became Academy Director before Jose Mourinho, then manager at Chelsea, asked him to become the youth coach at Stamford Bridge in 2004. That lasted until 2008 when he became manager of Watford before, just the following year, former club Reading tempted him back as manager. Just six months later Brendan left by mutual consent and moved to Swansea City in 2010 – a move which saw him become the first manager to lead a Welsh side to the Premier League. They finished 11th the following term and Liverpool came calling so he became manager at Anfield,

coming within a whisker of lifting the title with the Merseyside club in season 2013/14.

Brendan parted company with Liverpool in October 2015 and, when the Celtic manager job became available, he was very quickly named among the front-runners for the position. Indeed, he was No.1 on Celtic's radar and the five-in-a-row championship party in Paradise just carried on when Brendan's appointment was announced.

The Irishman was visibly moved as he was paraded as the club's 18th manager in front

of thousands of enthusiastic supporters on a memorable evening in Paradise. Like many of his countrymen, Brendan was reared on the Hoops, watching his heroes in action for the first time as an 11-year-old growing up in his native Carnlough. To be taking charge of the club he has always supported was an immensely proud moment for Brendan and sparked an emotional reaction within the Rodgers family.

Along with being a fan, Brendan Rodgers is well aware of Celtic's rich history, heritage and its legends, particularly Tommy Burns. As Brendan started his coaching journey as a youth coach in Reading in the late 1990s, Tommy Burns was in charge of the English club and he left a lasting impression on the new Hoops boss. To follow the likes of Tommy Burns, Jock Stein, Billy McNeill and all the other greats who have held the reigns in Paradise was special for him but it also increased his desire to emulate them and deliver success to the club.

SPOT THE DIFFERENCE

THERE are 10 differences in these pictures of Leigh Griffiths scoring against Ross County at Celtic Park. The first one has been circled, but can you spot the rest?

Answers on pages 62/63.

SPFL SEASON 2015/16 QUIZ

1. Which side did Celtic open their title defence against?

2. In how many league games did Logan Bailly replace Craig Gordon in goal?

3. Two teams scored own goals for Celtic; who were they?

4. Which side visited Celtic Park three times on league duty?

5. How many points did Celtic finish ahead of Aberdeen?

6. What was Celtic's highest-scoring game?

7. Which team failed to score against the Hoops?

8. Who scored the final goal of Celtic's campaign?

9. Which player was Celtic's second-top scorer?

10. Which Celt made the most substitute appearances?

Answers on page 62/63.

AUGUST

1	SPFL	2-0 v ROSS COUNTY	(GRIFFITHS [PEN], JOHANSEN)
9	SPFL	2-0 v PARTICK THISTLE	(ROGIC, COMMONS)
12	SPFL	2-2 v KILMARNOCK	(GRIFFITHS, BITTON)
15	SPFL	4-2 v INVERNESS CT	(LUSTIG, GRIFFITHS, ARMSTRONG [2])
22	SPFL	3-1 v DUNDEE UNITED	(GRIFFITHS, DURNAN [OG], McGREGOR)
29	SPFL	3-1 v ST JOHNSTONE	(GRIFFITHS, ROGIC, MULGREW)

CELTIC had an arduous start to the campaign, playing nine games in four weeks across Europe and Scotland in August and, although they started brightly, the month ended with their exit from the UEFA Champions League.

The Hoops opened the defence of their SPFL Premiership title with a convincing Flag Day win over Ross County, a highlight of which was the impressive home debut of defender Kieran Tierney.

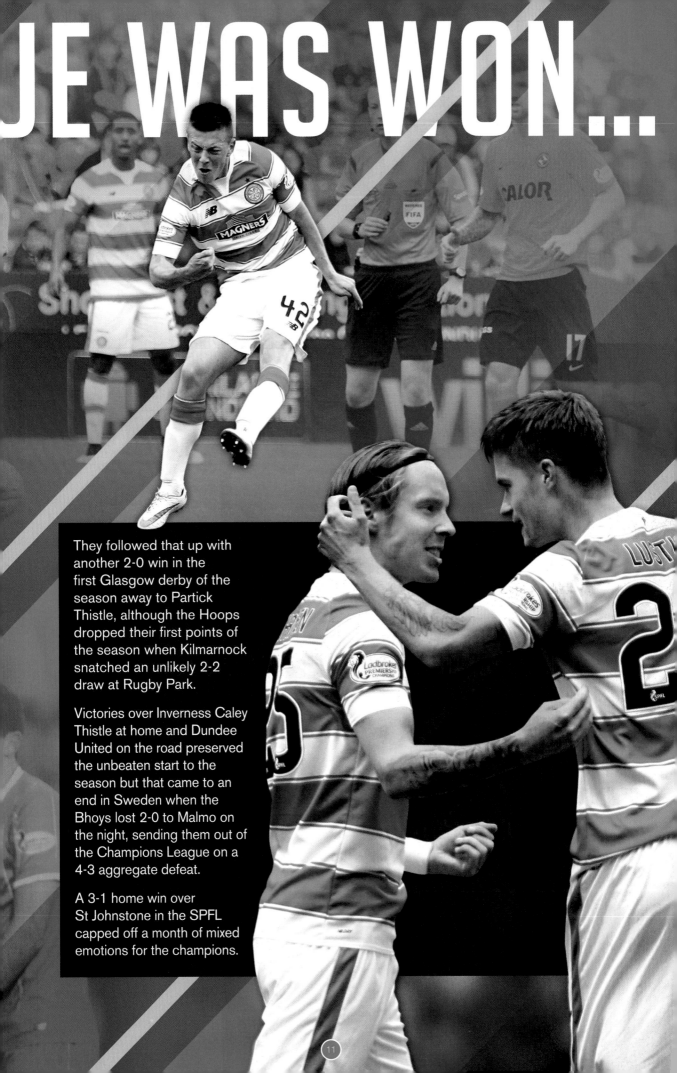

JE WAS WON...

They followed that up with another 2-0 win in the first Glasgow derby of the season away to Partick Thistle, although the Hoops dropped their first points of the season when Kilmarnock snatched an unlikely 2-2 draw at Rugby Park.

Victories over Inverness Caley Thistle at home and Dundee United on the road preserved the unbeaten start to the season but that came to an end in Sweden when the Bhoys lost 2-0 to Malmo on the night, sending them out of the Champions League on a 4-3 aggregate defeat.

A 3-1 home win over St Johnstone in the SPFL capped off a month of mixed emotions for the champions.

SEPTEMBER

THE Hoops only had three Premiership games in September but the trio of matches proved to be a mixed bag for Ronny Deila's side.

They began with a visit to Pittodrie to take on Aberdeen and found themselves on the end of a 2-1 defeat, despite taking the lead through a Leigh Griffiths penalty and the visitors finding themselves down to 10 men when Jonny Hayes was red-carded. A last-minute goal gave the home side a 2-1 win.

12	SPFL	1-2 v ABERDEEN	(GRIFFITHS)
20	SPFL	6-0 v DUNDEE	(ROGIC, GRIFFITHS, IZAGUIRRE (2), BROWN, CIFTCI)
26	SPFL	0-0 v HEARTS	

However, Celtic bounced back to record an emphatic 6-0 victory over Dundee at Celtic Park, with Emilio Izaguirre the unlikely two goal hero on the night. Indeed, he could have netted a hat-trick and gone home with the match ball, had he converted the penalty which his teammates had encouraged him to take. The other scorers on the night were Tom Rogic, Leigh Griffiths, Scott Brown and Nadir Ciftci.

Having lost one game and won another, the Hoops' final league fixture of the month was at home against Hearts. Despite creating a host of chances that could have won the game, the result was a goalless draw.

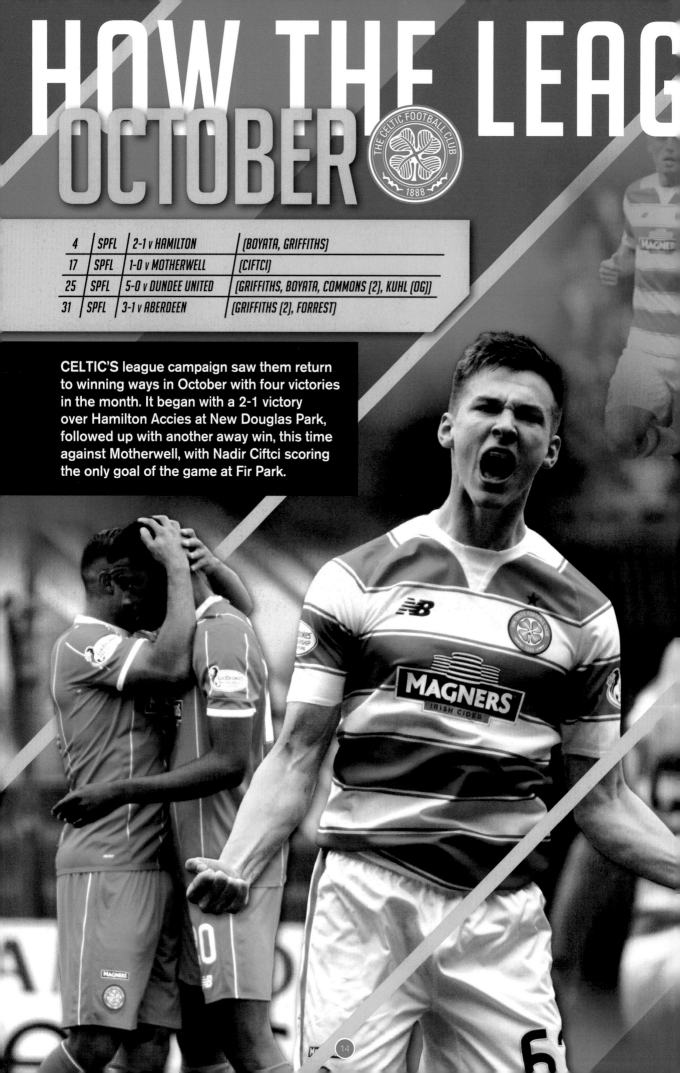

4	SPFL	2-1 v HAMILTON	(BOYATA, GRIFFITHS)
17	SPFL	1-0 v MOTHERWELL	(CIFTCI)
25	SPFL	5-0 v DUNDEE UNITED	(GRIFFITHS, BOYATA, COMMONS (2), KUHL (OG))
31	SPFL	3-1 v ABERDEEN	(GRIFFITHS (2), FORREST)

CELTIC'S league campaign saw them return to winning ways in October with four victories in the month. It began with a 2-1 victory over Hamilton Accies at New Douglas Park, followed up with another away win, this time against Motherwell, with Nadir Ciftci scoring the only goal of the game at Fir Park.

Premiership strugglers Dundee United visited Celtic Park towards the end of October and were duly thumped 5-0, with Kris Commons netting a double, while Leigh Griffiths continued his impressive form with another goal.

On the last day of the month, Celtic played host to Aberdeen and comprehensively beat their nearest title rivals. Leigh Griffiths headed the Hoops into the lead just before the break, rising high to direct Kieran Tierney's pinpoint cross into the back of the net. Celtic's No.9 then doubled his side's lead early in the second-half when he converted a penalty. James Forrest extended Celtic's lead on the hour mark, and Adam Rooney's last-minute goal was no more than a consolation strike for Derek McInnes' side.

CELTIC extended their unbeaten run in the league to nine games in November with an emphatic 4-1 victory over Ross County up in Dingwall. Tom Rogic's blistering strike from the edge of the box on 38 minutes gave the Hoops a first-half lead and a quick-fire double from Leigh Griffiths after the break put Celtic in control.

The home side briefly rallied and reduced the deficit, but a Nir Bitton strike ensured a comfortable afternoon for the Champions.

That win was followed by another day of frustration at Celtic Park however, as Kilmarnock managed to avoid defeat against the Hoops for the second consecutive time.

8	SPFL	4-1 v ROSS COUNTY	(ROGIC, GRIFFITHS (2), BITTON)
21	SPFL	0-0 v KILMARNOCK	
29	SPFL	3-1 v INVERNESS CT	(McGREGOR, GRIFFITHS, DEVINE (OG))

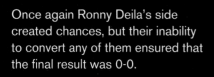

Once again Ronny Deila's side created chances, but their inability to convert any of them ensured that the final result was 0-0.

Having started November's league campaign with a trip to the Highlands, the Hoops ended the month in the same way, this time travelling to Inverness to take on Caley Thistle.

Callum McGregor gave Celtic an early lead but the home side levelled before the break. Leigh Griffiths once again made a decisive contribution, restoring Celtic's lead just before the hour mark, and an own goal from Daniel Devine made it 3-1 for Celtic's first away win over the Highland side since Ronny Deila took over.

DECEMBER

THE festive season had a false start for the Celts with their Premiership match against Hamilton on December 5 postponed due to the adverse weather, but when they did get their December fixtures underway, it was with a 3-0 victory over St Johnstone at McDiarmid Park. Nadir Ciftci hit a double in that game, while Dedryck Boyata also got on the scoresheet.

13	SPFL	3-0 v ST JOHNSTONE	(CIFTCI (2), BOYATA)
19	SPFL	1-2 v MOTHERWELL	(BITTON)
27	SPFL	2-2 v HEARTS	(BITTON, ROGIC)

UE WAS WON...

This was followed up with a disappointing 2-1 home defeat against Motherwell in their final league match of 2015, and their Premiership fixtures for the calendar year finished with a 2-2 draw against Hearts at Tynecastle, despite twice taking the lead. The home side snatched a point with a last-gasp goal.

There had been one further fixture scheduled before the turn of the year – away to Dundee on December 30 – but just as December had started with a postponed fixture, it ended with

one too as the match at Dens Park was postponed.

So, as Celtic entered 2016, they found themselves level with Aberdeen on 43 points, although the Hoops had played two games fewer than their title rivals, while their goal difference was already vastly superior.

2	SPFL	1-0 v PARTICK THISTLE	(GRIFFITHS)
15	SPFL	4-1 v DUNDEE UNITED	(GRIFFITHS (2), SIMUNOVIC, COMMONS)
19	SPFL	8-1 v HAMILTON	(GRIFFITHS (3), LUSTIG, BITTON, ROGIC, FORREST, McGREGOR)
23	SPFL	3-1 v ST JOHNSTONE	(MACKAY-STEVEN (2), ARMSTRONG)

CELTIC began 2016 with a Glasgow derby and it proved to be a tough game against a resolute Partick Thistle side. The Hoops were reduced to 10 men with just over 20 minutes of the match remaining when Nir Bitton was sent off and they had to rely on Leigh Griffiths, on as a half-time substitute for Nadir Ciftci, to provide the only goal of the game, the striker popping up with an injury-time winner.

Two weeks later, Griffiths hit a double as the Hoops beat Dundee United 4-1 at Tannadice. That game also saw Croatian defender Jozo Simunovic score his first goal for the Hoops while Kris Commons also chipped in with a spectacular volley.

Next up was a home game against Hamilton Accies and Griffiths went one better again as he scored a hat trick and went home with the match ball. It was an impressive performance from Ronny Deila's team, who recorded a comprehensive 8-1 victory over the Lanarkshire side. The other goalscorers were Mikael Lustig, Nir Bitton, Tom Rogic, James Forrest and Callum McGregor.

The month's league fixtures ended with another home win, this time a 3-1 victory over St Johnstone. Stuart Armstrong netted a goal in that game, while Gary Mackay-Steven hit a double.

Sadly, the month finished with League Cup disappointment at Hampden with Ross County knocking the cup holders out of the tournament with a 3-1 win, a match that saw January transfer-window signing Erik Sviatchenko make his debut.

FEBRUARY

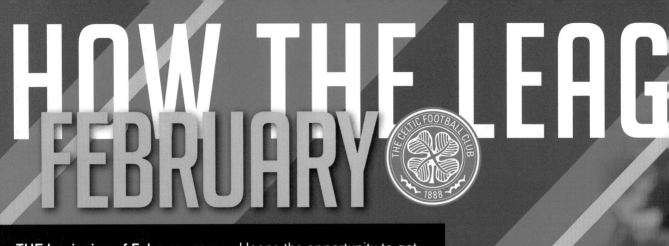

THE beginning of February saw a trip to Pittodrie and another 2-1 defeat at the hands of Aberdeen. Two first-half goals put the home side in control of the match with Celtic only reducing the deficit in the final minute through Leigh Griffiths.

Consecutive home games against the two Highland sides – Ross County and Inverness Caley Thistle – gave the

Hoops the opportunity to get back to winning ways and they did just that with a 2-0 win over Ross County, courtesy of goals from Leigh Griffiths and Dedryck Boyata, and a 3-0 win against Inverness Caley Thistle. Again, Griffiths was on target, this time with a double, while Gary Mackay-Steven also fired in a goal.

3	SPFL	1-2 v ABERDEEN	(GRIFFITHS)
13	SPFL	2-0 v ROSS COUNTY	(GRIFFITHS, BOYATA)
20	SPFL	3-0 v INVERNESS CT	(GRIFFITHS (2), MACKAY-STEVEN)
26	SPFL	1-1 v HAMILTON	(GRIFFITHS)

UE WAS WON...

The month ended with Friday night football against Hamilton Accies at New Douglas Park and it proved to be a frustrating night for Ronny Deila's side. Leigh Griffiths (who else!) gave the Hoops the lead in the 35th minute, but just before half-time Dedryck Boyata was red-carded. The home side managed to capitalise on the numerical advantage, scoring an equaliser through Eamonn Brophy on 73 minutes.

MARCH

2	SPFL	0-0 v DUNDEE	
12	SPFL	2-1 v PARTICK THISTLE	(GRIFFITHS, McGREGOR)
19	SPFL	1-0 v KILMARNOCK	(ROGIC)

CELTIC only played three league games in the month of March and it began with a very disappointing goalless draw at home to Dundee. Patrick Roberts, who joined on an 18-month loan from Manchester City in January, made his first start for the Hoops and looked lively, but it was a less than vintage performance from the Hoops.

Another Glasgow derby followed 10 days later and this time Celtic did manage to hit the target. Top goalscorer Leigh Griffiths opened the scoring on the stroke of half-time before Callum McGregor doubled Celtic's lead with an impressive run and finish early in the second-half.

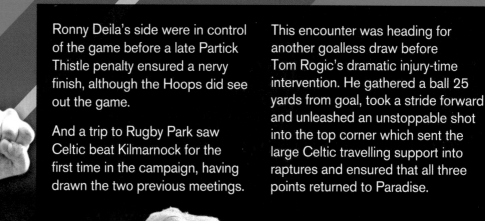

Ronny Deila's side were in control of the game before a late Partick Thistle penalty ensured a nervy finish, although the Hoops did see out the game.

And a trip to Rugby Park saw Celtic beat Kilmarnock for the first time in the campaign, having drawn the two previous meetings.

This encounter was heading for another goalless draw before Tom Rogic's dramatic injury-time intervention. He gathered a ball 25 yards from goal, took a stride forward and unleashed an unstoppable shot into the top corner which sent the large Celtic travelling support into raptures and ensured that all three points returned to Paradise.

APRIL

2	SPFL	3-1 v HEARTS	(ROBERTS (2), MACKAY-STEVEN)
5	SPFL	0-0 v DUNDEE	
9	SPFL	2-1 v MOTHERWELL	(GRIFFITHS (2))
24	SPFL	1-1 v ROSS COUNTY	(GRIFFITHS)
30	SPFL	3-1 v HEARTS	(KAZIM-RICHARDS, ROBERTS, GRIFFITHS)

CELTIC faced a tough fixture at the start of April as Hearts were the visitors to Paradise but, in the event, Ronny Deila's side produced a convincing performance to win the match 3-1, despite going a goal down when Jamie Walker scored a blistering opener from 25 yards out.

Gary Mackay-Steven equalised with a powerful drive from the edge of the box after 15 minutes, but it was winger Patrick Roberts who hit the headlines with his first two goals for the club. He latched on to a Tom Rogic through ball to give Celtic the lead, coolly chipping the onrushing Hearts goalkeeper.

And he scored another impressive goal in the second-half to extend Celtic's lead, cutting in from the right before unleashing a precise left-foot shot into the back of the net.

Having produced an impressive performance, the Hoops followed that up with a disappointing goalless draw against Dundee at Dens Park in the fixture that was rearranged from the end of December, but they returned to winning ways the following weekend with a 2-1 victory over Motherwell, with Leigh Griffiths netting a double.

A frustrating 1-1 draw at home to Ross County followed the

previous weekend's Scottish Cup semi-final exit, but results had conspired to mean that victory in the final league game of April - against Hearts at Tynecastle - would effectively seal the title, with Celtic's vastly superior goal difference making it well-nigh impossible for Aberdeen to catch them.

And it was another impressive Celtic performance against Hearts. Colin Kazim-Richards scored his first league goal for the club on 17 minutes with an excellent finish at the back post and, although the home side equalised early in the second-half, it was the Hoops who went on to win the match.

Patrick Roberts restored Celtic's lead just after the hour mark with a cool finish before Leigh Griffiths pressurised the Hearts defence into making a mistake that he capitalised on to fire home Celtic's third goal of the day and his 39th of the campaign.

It sparked celebrations in the stadium between players, fans and management who knew that barring a disaster of biblical proportions, a fifth consecutive league title was heading to Paradise.

MAY

THE CELTIC FOOTBALL CLUB
1888

CELTIC only needed one point to confirm their status as five-in-a-row champions when they faced second-place Aberdeen at Celtic Park but, in the event, they took all three in an entertaining match.

Patrick Roberts was the star of the show with two goals on the day. His first goal was a spectacular effort, cutting in from the right flank before firing home an unstoppable shot from 25 yards out.

His second goal was an equally impressive finish. Leigh Griffiths threaded a ball through for the Englishman and, from the edge of the box, he curled a left-foot shot beyond the Aberdeen goalkeeper.

And when Mikael Lustig made it 3-0 just after half-time following good work from Callum McGregor, Celtic were in cruise control. However, two lapses in concentration allowed Aberdeen to reduce the deficit but the Hoops held firm to win the match 3-2 and secure an impressive fifth league title in a row.

The players and management took a well-deserved lap of honour in front of the celebrating Celtic support, something that was replicated when the SPFL Premiership trophy was presented to the Champions.

Celtic's penultimate league game of the campaign saw them visit McDiarmid Park to take on St Johnstone. And

Leigh Griffiths gave the Hoops the lead just after half-time with a brilliant individual goal which represented his 40th strike of a remarkable season. Unfortunately, two defensive mistakes allowed St Johnstone to capitalise and win the match 2-1, although it could not take away from Griffiths' tremendous goalscoring achievement, or the debut of 17-year-old defender Anthony Ralston who came on at right-back in the second-half.

There was even more debut delight when Motherwell

8	SPFL	3-2 v ABERDEEN	(ROBERTS (2), LUSTIG)
11	SPFL	1-2 v ST JOHNSTONE	(GRIFFITHS)
15	SPFL	7-0 v MOTHERWELL	(TIERNEY, ROGIC, LUSTIG, ARMSTRONG, ROBERTS, CHRISTIE, AITCHISON)

arrived as opposition on trophy day, as the Hoops went into overdrive with a 7-0 win.

The rout was started when Kieran Tierney scored his first ever goal for Celtic while Tom Rogic and Mikael Lustig added theirs before the half-hour mark.

Stuart Armstrong and Patrick Roberts also scored before Ryan Christie got off the mark with his first goal for the club to make it 6-0.

Then, just two minutes after coming on as a sub to be Celtic's youngest ever debutant, 16-year-old Jack Aitchison, scored with his first ever touch of the ball as a senior player to automatically also become the club's youngest ever scorer.

Then the party began in earnest as, on the sunniest of sunny days, Scott Brown raised the SPFL trophy high in Paradise for the fifth consecutive season.

Ladbrokes PREMIERSHIP 2015/16 CHAMPIONS

MAZE

WHEN manager Brendan Rodgers arrived at the portals of Paradise on his first day, he had to find his way from the main entrance through to the hallowed turf where 13,000 supporters were waiting.

Can you help him make his way through the inner sanctum of Celtic Park to greet the faithful for the first time?

Find out how Brendan made his way to the fans on pages 62/63.

START

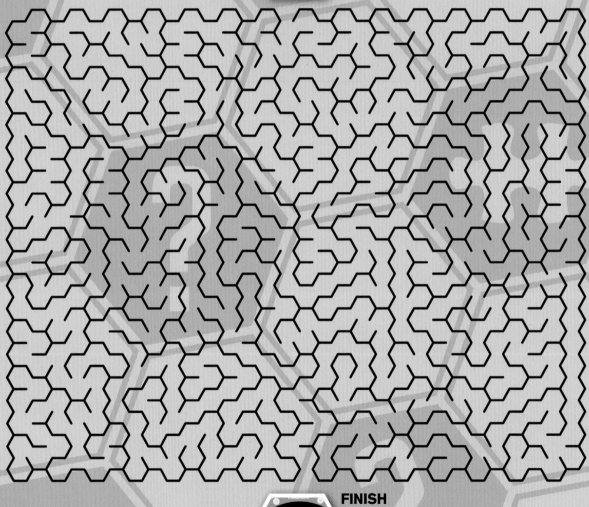

FINISH

CROSSWORD

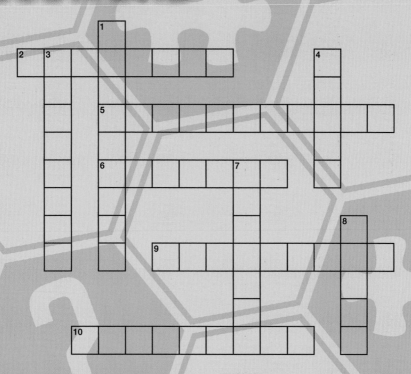

ACROSS

2. Lisbon club who wear the Hoops. (8)

5. Celtic's Danish defender. (11)

6. Our manager's surname. (7)

9. The previous club of Celtic's manager. (9)

10. The club's youngest scorer. (9)

DOWN

1. Joined Celtic from Dundee United. (9)

3. Celtic Park is also known as _____. (8)

4. He has a Swiss role at Celtic. (5)

7. An English Celt on the wing. (7)

8. We want to see the Hoops score loads of these. (5)

QUIZ

1. How many league titles have Celtic won?

2. Which club did Celtic play their first competitive match against last season?

3. How many club legends are on the banners at each side of Celtic Park?

4. Who made the most appearances for Celtic last season?

5. Which two countries did Celtic visit on European duty for the first time in season 2015/16?

Check out the answers on pages 62/63.

WORDS OF WISDOM
WHAT THE CELTS WOULD TELL THEIR YOUNGER SELVES

EVERY young player has to start somewhere and they will always be getting plenty of advice from parents, relations, friends, teachers, coaches and many more as they start out on their career.

However, what if we could turn back the clock and get the Celtic players to give their younger selves some guidance in their careers?

That's exactly what we did and we got some interesting answers from these Celts.

CALLUM McGREGOR

I would tell myself to keep being positive, keep working hard all the time on your technique and always practise. When I was a young kid I was always practising and training. Even when I went home, I would go outside in the garden doing my keepy-ups and hitting the ball against the wall and controlling it. So I would say practise all the time and believe that you are as good as anyone and that you can achieve your targets.

KIERAN TIERNEY

My advice would be to always try to enjoy what you do. You don't want to wake up going to training not looking forward to it. You need to realise how lucky you are and how much people would give to be in your position so you need to give it your all every time you're on the pitch, both at training and in games. My family always tell me I'm lucky to be where I am, but I deserve it too as I've worked hard. You need to be grateful and keep level-headed because it can change quickly and you need to make the most of every minute.

TOM ROGIC

I feel that hard work is the most important thing. You can be talented but nothing comes easy and you have to earn everything. Hard work would be the main thing. You have your setbacks, as I've had, but you need to be mentally strong and keep working hard and you'll get the reward in the end.

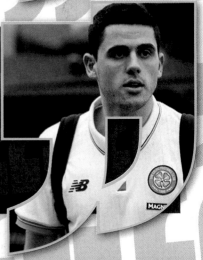

SAIDY JANKO

I don't really regret anything, but I would just say don't pretend anything. Be who you are. That's what I did. It brought me here and I think that's not too bad.

EMILIO IZAGUIRRE

My advice to my younger self would be to always be professional. Enjoy life every day and respect it. Respect God and other people. Love what you do for a living.

LUKE DONNELLY

I would say, have no regrets and don't play with any fear. Just go out there and express yourself rather than think about how big the game is. Don't let the pressure get to you and just take it as it comes.

STUART ARMSTRONG

I would tell myself just don't worry about things too much and be confident.

For more Words of Wisdom, see pages 56-57.

PLAYER PROFILES

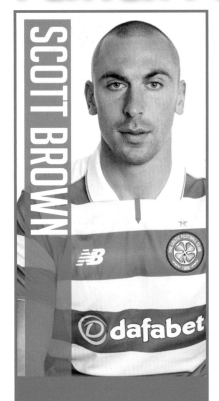

SCOTT BROWN

POSITION: MIDFIELDER
SQUAD NUMBER: 8
D.O.B: 25/06/85
BORN: HILL O' BEATH, SCOTLAND
HEIGHT: 5'10"
SIGNED: 01/07/07
DEBUT: V KILMARNOCK (H) 0-0, (SPL) 05/08/07
PREVIOUS CLUBS: HIBERNIAN

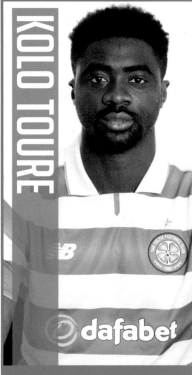

KOLO TOURE

POSITION: DEFENDER
SQUAD NUMBER: 2
D.O.B: 19/03/81
BORN: BOUAKE, IVORY COAST
HEIGHT: 5' 10"
SIGNED: 24/07/16
DEBUT: V ASTANA (H) 2-1, (UCL) 03/08/16
PREVIOUS CLUBS: LIVERPOOL, MANCHESTER CITY, ARSENAL, ASEC MIMOSAS

SCOTT SINCLAIR

POSITION: MIDFIELDER
SQUAD NUMBER: 11
D.O.B: 25/03/89
BORN: BATH, ENGLAND
HEIGHT: 5' 10"
SIGNED: 07/08/16
DEBUT: V HEARTS (A) 2-1, (SPFL) 07/08/16
PREVIOUS CLUBS: ASTON VILLA, ASTON VILLA (LOAN), WEST BROMWICH ALBION (LOAN), MANCHESTER CITY, SWANSEA CITY, WIGAN ATHLETIC (LOAN), BIRMINGHAM CITY (LOAN), CRYSTAL PALACE (LOAN), CHARLTON ATHLETIC (LOAN), QUEENS PARK RANGERS (LOAN), PLYMOUTH ARGYLE (LOAN), CHELSEA, BRISTOL ROVERS

MOUSSA DEMBELE

POSITION: STRIKER
SQUAD NUMBER: 10
D.O.B: 12/07/96
BORN: POINTOISE, FRANCE
HEIGHT: 6' 0"
SIGNED: 01/07/16
DEBUT: V LINCOLN RED IMPS (A) 0-1, (UCL) 12/07/16
PREVIOUS CLUBS: FULHAM, PARIS SAINT-GERMAIN

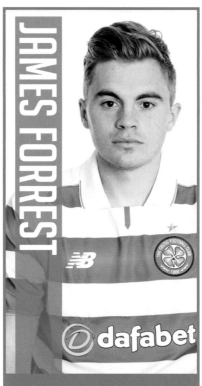

JAMES FORREST

POSITION: MIDFIELDER
SQUAD NUMBER: 49
D.O.B: 07/07/91
BORN: GLASGOW, SCOTLAND
HEIGHT: 5' 9"
SIGNED: 01/07/09
DEBUT: v MOTHERWELL (H) 4-0, (SPL) 01/05/10
PREVIOUS CLUBS: CELTIC YOUTH

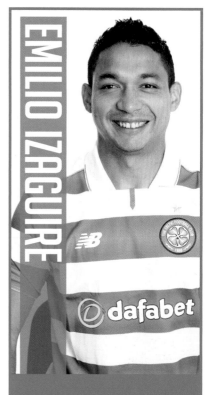

EMILIO IZAGUIRE

POSITION: DEFENDER
SQUAD NUMBER: 3
D.O.B: 10/05/86
BORN: TEGUCIGALPA, HONDURAS
HEIGHT: 5' 8"
SIGNED: 18/08/10
DEBUT: v MOTHERWELL (A) 1-0, (SPL) 29/08/10
PREVIOUS CLUBS: MOTAGUA

PLAYER PROFILES

KRIS COMMONS

POSITION: MIDFIELDER
SQUAD NUMBER: 15
D.O.B: 30/08/83
BORN: NOTTINGHAM, ENGLAND
HEIGHT: 5' 6"
SIGNED: 28/01/11
DEBUT: v ABERDEEN (H) 4-1, (CIS) 29/01/11
PREVIOUS CLUBS: DERBY COUNTY, NOTTINGHAM FOREST, STOKE CITY

TOM ROGIC

POSITION: MIDFIELDER
SQUAD NUMBER: 18
D.O.B: 16/12/92
BORN: GRIFFITH, AUSTRALIA
HEIGHT: 6' 2"
SIGNED: 09/01/13
DEBUT: v INVERNESS CALEY THISTLE (A) 3-1, (SPL) 09/02/13
PREVIOUS CLUBS: CENTRAL COAST MARINERS, BELCONNEN UNITED, ANU FC

EFE AMBROSE

POSITION: DEFENDER
SQUAD NUMBER: 4
D.O.B: 18/10/88
BORN: KADUNA, NIGERIA
HEIGHT: 6' 3"
SIGNED: 31/08/12
DEBUT: v DUNDEE (H) 2-0, (SPL) 22/09/12
PREVIOUS CLUBS: FC ASHDOD, BAYELSA UNITED (LOAN), KADUNA UNITED

NIR BITTON

POSITION: MIDFIELDER
SQUAD NUMBER: 6
D.O.B: 30/10/91
BORN: ASHDOD, ISRAEL
HEIGHT: 6' 5"
SIGNED: 30/08/13
DEBUT: v AC MILAN (A) 0-2, (UCL) 18/09/13
PREVIOUS CLUBS: FC ASHDOD

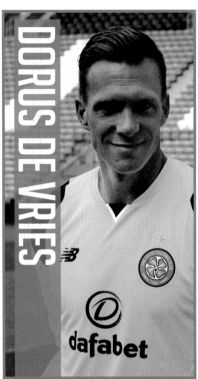

DORUS DE VRIES

POSITION: GOALKEEPER
SQUAD NUMBER: 24
D.O.B: 29/12/80
BORN: BEVERWIJK, NETHERLANDS
HEIGHT: 6' 1"
SIGNED: 24/07/16
DEBUT: v ABERDEEN (H) 4-1, (SPFL) 27/08/16
PREVIOUS CLUBS: NOTTINGHAM FOREST, WOLVERHAMPTON WANDERERS, SWANSEA CITY, DUNFERMLINE, ADO DEN HAAG, TELSTAR

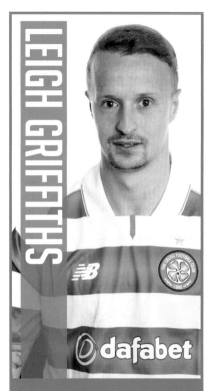

LEIGH GRIFFITHS

POSITION: STRIKER
SQUAD NUMBER: 9
D.O.B: 20/08/90
BORN: EDINBURGH, SCOTLAND
HEIGHT: 5' 8"
SIGNED: 31/01/14
DEBUT: v ABERDEEN (A) 1-2, (SPL) 08/02/14
PREVIOUS CLUBS: WOLVERHAMPTON WANDERERS, HIBERNIAN (LOAN), DUNDEE, LIVINGSTON

PLAYER PROFILES

EOGHAN O'CONNELL

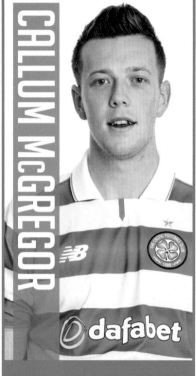

CALLUM McGREGOR

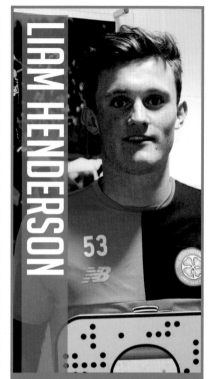

LIAM HENDERSON

POSITION: DEFENDER
SQUAD NUMBER: 34
D.O.B: 13/08/95
BORN: CORK, IRELAND
HEIGHT: 6' 2"
SIGNED: 14/02/14
DEBUT: v ROSS COUNTY (H) 1-1, (SPFL) 29/03/14
PREVIOUS CLUBS: CELTIC YOUTH

POSITION: MIDFIELDER
SQUAD NUMBER: 42
D.O.B: 14/06/93
BORN: GLASGOW, SCOTLAND
HEIGHT: 5' 9"
SIGNED: 07/07/09
DEBUT: v KR REYKJAVIK (A) 1-0, (UCL) 15/07/14
PREVIOUS CLUBS: CELTIC YOUTH

POSITION: MIDFIELDER
SQUAD NUMBER: 53
D.O.B: 25/04/96
BORN: LIVINGSTON, SCOTLAND
HEIGHT: 6' 0"
SIGNED: 31/07/13
DEBUT: v MOTHERWELL (A) 5-0, (SPFL) 06/12/13
PREVIOUS CLUBS: CELTIC YOUTH

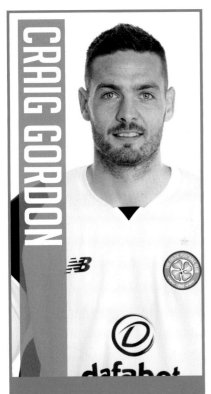

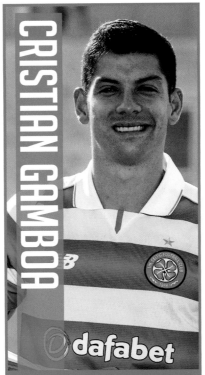

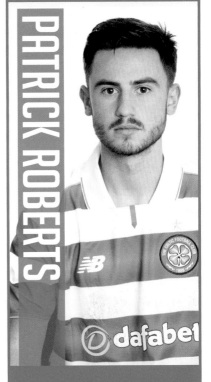

CRAIG GORDON

POSITION: GOALKEEPER

SQUAD NUMBER: 1

D.O.B: 31/12/82

BORN: EDINBURGH, SCOTLAND

HEIGHT: 6' 4"

SIGNED: 03/07/14

DEBUT: V ST JOHNSTONE (A) 3-0, (SPFL) 13/08/14

PREVIOUS CLUBS: SUNDERLAND, HEARTS, COWDENBEATH (LOAN)

CRISTIAN GAMBOA

POSITION: DEFENDER

SQUAD NUMBER: 12

D.O.B: 24/10/89

BORN: LIBERIA, COSTA RICA

HEIGHT: 5' 8"

SIGNED: 30/08/16

DEBUT: V N/A

PREVIOUS CLUBS: WEST BROMWICH ALBION, ROSENBORG, ROSENBORG (LOAN), COPENHAGEN, FREDRIKSTAD, MUNICIPAL LIBERIA

PATRICK ROBERTS

POSITION: MIDFIELDER

SQUAD NUMBER: 27

D.O.B: 05/02/97

BORN: KINGSTON UPON THAMES, ENGLAND

HEIGHT: 5' 6"

SIGNED: 01/02/16

DEBUT: v INVERNESS CALEY THISTLE (H) 3-0, (SPFL) 20/02/16

PREVIOUS CLUBS: MANCHESTER CITY, FULHAM

PLAYER PROFILES

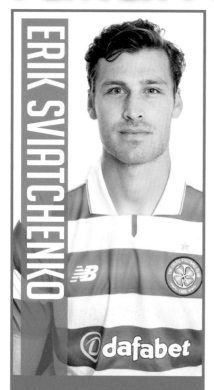

ERIK SVIATCHENKO

POSITION: DEFENDER
SQUAD NUMBER: 28
D.O.B: 04/10/91
BORN: VIBORG, DENMARK
HEIGHT: 6' 1"
SIGNED: 17/01/16
DEBUT: v ROSS COUNTY (N) 1-3, (LEAGUE CUP) 31/01/16
PREVIOUS CLUBS: FC MIDTJYLLAND

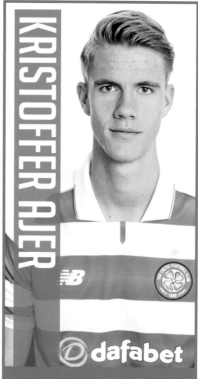

KRISTOFFER AJER

POSITION: MIDFIELDER
SQUAD NUMBER: 35
D.O.B: 07/04/98
BORN: NORWAY
HEIGHT: 6' 5"
SIGNED: 17/02/16
DEBUT: v LINCOLN RED IMPS (H) 3-0 (UCL) 20/07/16
PREVIOUS CLUBS: IK START

SAIDY JANKO

POSITION: DEFENDER
SQUAD NUMBER: 22
D.O.B: 22/11/95
BORN: ZURICH, SWITZERLAND
HEIGHT: 5' 10"
SIGNED: 01/07/15
DEBUT: v ROSS COUNTY (H) 2-0, (SPFL) 01/08/2015
PREVIOUS CLUBS: BOLTON WANDERERS (LOAN), MANCHESTER UNITED

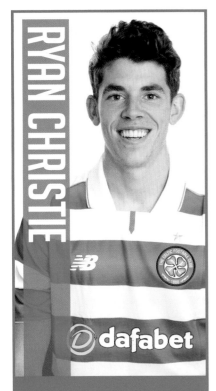

RYAN CHRISTIE

POSITION: MIDFIELDER
SQUAD NUMBER: 17
D.O.B: 22/02/95
BORN: INVERNESS, SCOTLAND
HEIGHT: 5' 10"
SIGNED: 01/09/15
DEBUT: v ST JOHNSTONE (H) 3-1, (SPFL) 23/01/16
PREVIOUS CLUBS: INVERNESS CALEY THISTLE

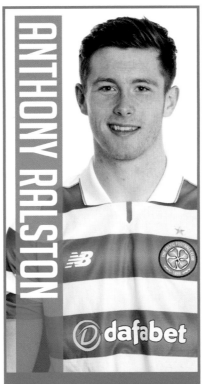

ANTHONY RALSTON

POSITION: DEFENDER
SQUAD NUMBER: 56
D.O.B: 16/11/98
BORN: AIRDRIE, SCOTLAND
HEIGHT: 5' 11"
SIGNED: 16/11/08
DEBUT: v ST JOHNSTONE (A) 1-2, (SPFL) 11/05/16
PREVIOUS CLUBS: CELTIC YOUTH

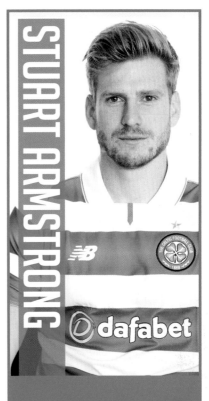

STUART ARMSTRONG

POSITION: MIDFIELDER
SQUAD NUMBER: 14
D.O.B: 30/03/92
BORN: INVERNESS, SCOTLAND
HEIGHT: 6' 0"
SIGNED: 02/02/15
DEBUT: v PARTICK THISTLE (A) 3-0, (SPFL) 11/02/15
PREVIOUS CLUBS: DUNDEE UNITED

PLAYER PROFILES

NADIR CIFTCI

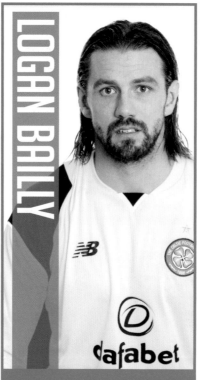

LOGAN BAILLY

LEO FASAN

POSITION: STRIKER
SQUAD NUMBER: 7
D.O.B: 02/02/92
BORN: KARAKOCAN, TURKEY
HEIGHT: 6' 1"
SIGNED: 09/07/15
DEBUT: v FC STJARNAN (H) 2-0, (UCL) 15/07/15
PREVIOUS CLUBS: DUNDEE UNITED, NAC BREDA, KAYSERISPOR, PORTSMOUTH

POSITION: GOALKEEPER
SQUAD NUMBER: 26
D.O.B: 27/12/85
BORN: LIEGE, BELGIUM
HEIGHT: 6' 3"
SIGNED: 08/07/15
DEBUT: v DUNDEE UNITED (A) 3-1, (SPFL) 22/08/15
PREVIOUS CLUBS: OH LEUVEN, NEUCHATEL XAMAX (LOAN), BORUSSIA MONCHENGLADBACH, HEUSDEN-ZOLDER (LOAN), GENK

POSITION: GOALKEEPER
SQUAD NUMBER: 38
D.O.B: 04/01/94
BORN: SAN VITO AL TAGLIAMENTO, ITALY
HEIGHT: 6' 2"
SIGNED: 14/02/14
DEBUT: N/A
PREVIOUS CLUBS: UDINESE (YOUTH)

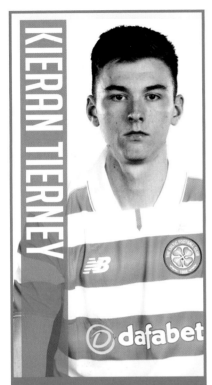

KIERAN TIERNEY

POSITION: DEFENDER
SQUAD NUMBER: 63
D.O.B: 05/06/97
BORN: DOUGLAS, ISLE OF MAN
HEIGHT: 5' 10"
SIGNED: 14/02/14
DEBUT: v DUNDEE (A) 2-1, (SPFL) 22/04/15
PREVIOUS CLUBS: CELTIC YOUTH

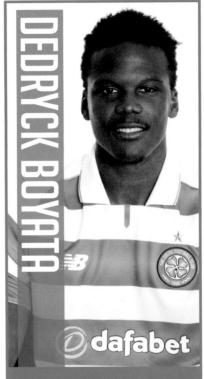

DEDRYCK BOYATA

POSITION: DEFENDER
SQUAD NUMBER: 20
D.O.B: 28/11/90
BORN: BRUSSELS, BELGIUM
HEIGHT: 6' 2"
SIGNED: 02/06/15
DEBUT: v FC STJARNAN (H) 2-0, (UCL) 15/07/15
PREVIOUS CLUBS: FC TWENTE (LOAN), BOLTON (LOAN), MANCHESTER CITY

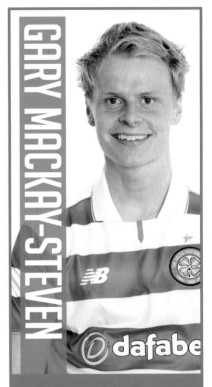

GARY MACKAY-STEVEN

POSITION: MIDFIELDER
SQUAD NUMBER: 16
D.O.B: 31/08/90
BORN: THURSO, SCOTLAND
HEIGHT: 5' 9"
SIGNED: 02/02/15
DEBUT: v PARTICK THISTLE (A) 3-0, (SPFL) 11/02/15
PREVIOUS CLUBS: AIRDRIE UNITED, DUNDEE UNITED

JOBS FOR THE BHOYS

What would your favourite stars be doing if they weren't footballers?

EVER since you could first talk, people have been asking: what do you want to be when you grow up?

It carries on through school when teachers and careers officers will be asking: what do you want to do when you leave school?

Well, we've turned the tables slightly by asking the players what they would be if they weren't footballers.

Would they have taken up something they were good at in school, or would they have followed in their father's footsteps?

Kris Commons

I don't know if I'd pick a specific job as I like to hang about with my pals and brother. I'd get into something that they do. My brother's an electrician so he's up and down the country doing work, so it'd be good craic to spend a lot of time with him. One of my closest friends is a funeral director so it'd be interesting to be involved with that. The finer details of a job like that go such a long way with people.

Craig Gordon

When I was at school my best subject was geography so something to do with that. We had a great geography teacher at Balerno High School, Miss McDevitt, so that probably helped make the subject more enjoyable.

Kieran Tierney

I would probably be an apprentice in the building trade. I wasn't the brainiest at school but I'd probably do an apprenticeship as a bricklayer.

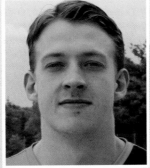

Luke Donnelly

Probably just a run-of-the-mill guy, working nine-to-five just trying to get by and working in an office somewhere.

Gary Mackay-Steven

I got asked this before and I said a zookeeper but I think I just pulled that out of thin air. I don't know what I'd be. I left school at 15 and it has always been football so I've never thought about a different career but I really like music so maybe I would have gone to University and studied music or sport.

Nir Bitton

That's a very difficult question but I'll give you the answer that my parents would want me to answer. If I wasn't a footballer, I think I'd have studied to become a lawyer, but I don't think that's ever going to happen now... or maybe a journalist!

Aidan Nesbitt

I'd be signing on. Monday morning. I'd maybe do more education or work with my Dad. I'm not qualified for anything else and I've never wanted to do anything else other than football, so I'm quite lucky.

For more Jobs For The Bhoys, see pages 52/53.

COLOURING-IN

WE want you to get out your crayons, ink markers or paints and bring this trio of Bhoys to full Celtic technicolour.

GUESS WHO?

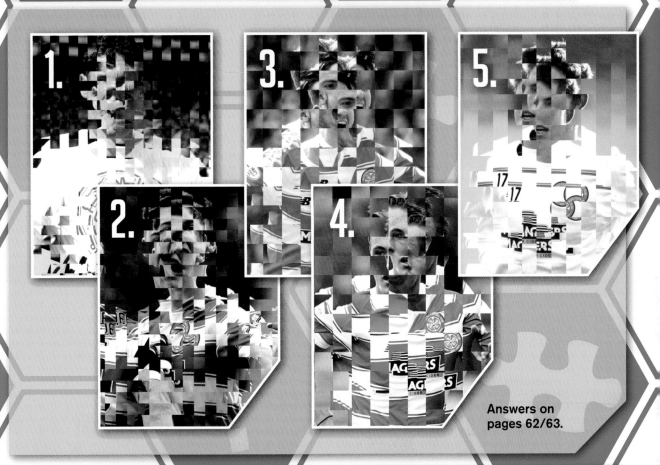

1.
2.
3.
4.
5.

Answers on pages 62/63.

FIVE-IN-A-ROW CHAMPIONEES

CELTIC finished the 2015/16 season as history makers after they clinched the SPFL Premiership title for the fifth time in a row.

Only two other Celtic teams in the past had achieved the great feat and Ronny Deila's side became the first in 45 years to do so, securing the top trophy in Scotland with a 3-2 win over Aberdeen at Paradise on May 8.

The season started in strong fashion but the Celts endured a difficult start to September, losing to Aberdeen before a rousing 6-0 win over Dundee sparked a turnaround before the end of the month and the Hoops continued to gain momentum in the league, finishing October with a 3-1 victory over Aberdeen, our closest rivals.

As the season entered its final third, March finished with a nail-biting 1-0 victory over Kilmarnock at Rugby Park, which heralded a turning point in the title race.

Aberdeen had been trailing Celtic closely all season but Tom Rogic's thunderous last-minute winner against Killie proved decisive as the Dons dropped points later that day against Motherwell, missing the chance to keep the heat on the champions.

The Celts finished April undefeated in the league, although they dropped out of the Scottish Cup at the semi-final, then came the news that Ronny Deila would be leaving the club at the end of the season.

The news of his departure was followed up with a frustrating 1-1 draw with Ross County, but Celtic finished the month with a massive 3-1 away win over Hearts, which all but secured the title.

The club was in a celebratory mood and the party continued as the Bhoys hosted Aberdeen the following week at Paradise where a 3-2 win finally clinched the trophy and sealed five-in-a-row.

The Celts then travelled to St Johnstone where, despite losing 2-1, fans witnessed the debut of youngster Anthony Ralston, as well as Leigh Griffiths' 40th goal of the season, before the campaign came to an emphatic close with the 7-0 destruction of Motherwell on trophy day on May 15.

The goals came from a magnificent seven different scorers including Kieran Tierney, who finished his outstanding season with his first goal for the club, while 16-year-old Jack Aitchison capped off a history-making campaign for Celtic by becoming the Hoops' youngest-ever debutant and scorer with the final goal of the day.

It was a fitting send-off for Ronny Deila and it left Paradise in delight after a tough but ultimately successful season.

Ladbrokes PREMIERSHIP

2015/16 CHAMPIONS

CELTIC FOOTBALL CLUB

GRADUATION IN GREEN AND WHITE

JUDGING by the performances and trophy successes of the teams at the top end of the Celtic Youth Academy pyramid over the past 12 months, the future looks bright in Paradise.

The Development Side, having lost out on the league title for the first time in five years in 2015, were determined to reassert their dominance of the division and they did so in scintillating style.

Not only did the Bhoys storm to the championship with seven games remaining in the season, but they achieved the remarkable feat of going through the whole campaign without defeat.

It was a wonderful effort from Tommy McIntyre and his young players and they richly deserved the ovation they received from the Celtic support when they paraded the trophy in Paradise at half-time during the 3-2 win over Aberdeen in May.

Another piece of silverware the young Celts had ambitions of holding aloft again was the

SFA Youth Cup, but a fourth round defeat away to St Johnstone ended their hopes.

The Hoops youngsters were also involved in prestigious international competitions in the form of the UEFA Youth League and the Premier League International Cup.

In the UEFA Youth League, after excellent wins over HJK Helsinki (6-1 on aggregate) and Puskas Akademia (3-1 on aggregate), they advanced into a play-off with Valencia, with the victors advancing to the last 16.

With several senior players out on loan, it was a youthful Hoops team that lined up against the talented Spaniards inside Celtic Park, yet they refused to be deterred, taking the game to the visitors.

And McIntyre's young guns looked on course for a stunning success when the then 15-year-old Jack Aitchison, one of four Celtic Youth Academy players to make their top-team bow during the season, fired them into a first-half lead. There would be heartbreak for the hosts, however, as they conceded a late equaliser and then lost out on the lottery of penalty kicks.

Up against more experienced opponents in the Premier League International Cup, Celtic failed to progress out of their group, which contained Benfica, Chelsea and Liverpool, but nonetheless it was another valuable experience for the young players.

At U17 level, there was double delight again for the youths. They produced a dazzling display to retain the Glasgow Cup, with a fantastic 4-0 win over Rangers in the final at Ibrox, thanks to goals from Michael Johnston, Broque Watson, Shaun Bowers and Kieran Patrick Campbell.

And, on the last day of the season, they secured the league championship in style, hammering title rivals Hamilton 5-0 at Lennoxtown, with Aitchison grabbing a hat-trick. Significantly, this success also guaranteed Celtic's participation in the UEFA Youth League in the following campaign.

JOBS FOR THE BHOYS

What would your favourite stars be doing if they weren't footballers?

ON pages 44/45, we had the first instalment of Jobs For The Bhoys and we now follow that up with some more thoughts from the Celtic players.

So, could you see Kieran Tierney as a bricklayer or Kris Commons as an electrician? Find out what more of the Celts would have in line if they hadn't taken up football.

Saidy Janko

I'd probably be working in Tesco! I'm not great at too many things. I did alright at school but I wasn't into too much. Now I'm into fashion so I'd maybe work in a fashion store or something. Perhaps I'd be a designer, or a model. Or both, like Kanye West.

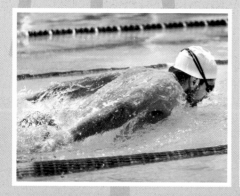

Tom Rogic

Some sort of athlete or sports related work. I enjoyed a lot of sports when I was younger so something like that.

Stuart Armstrong

I'd probably have studied law. I started studying law at a time when I wasn't always in the team or the First 11, so sometimes I'd come home and have a lot of free time. It made me feel like I was doing something worthwhile when I did it and when I was at school I thought about doing something along those lines.

Emilio Izaguirre

I'd probably be an electrical engineer. I studied for that and my Dad did the same and now he's a teacher.

Eoghan O'Connell

I was alright at school but I'd probably have tried to play Gaelic or hurling for Cork. That'd have been the dream if I wasn't here.

Scott Brown

It's got to be something to do with sport. I've got so much energy I need to use it somewhere. If I didn't I'd probably be huge! I'm not a suit and tie guy. I'm more of a scruffy looking guy so probably something to do with sport. I quite enjoy the coaching with the Under-20s so I'd probably still try to get into that.

Callum McGregor

I have been asked this a lot of times and I can never really give them an answer. I have been involved in sport and football all my days and I quite like sports science side of things, so maybe if I wasn't a footballer I would try and go down that avenue.

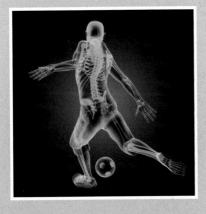

DOT-TO-DOT

JOIN up all of the dots in this picture and see if you can identify what the Celtic image is.

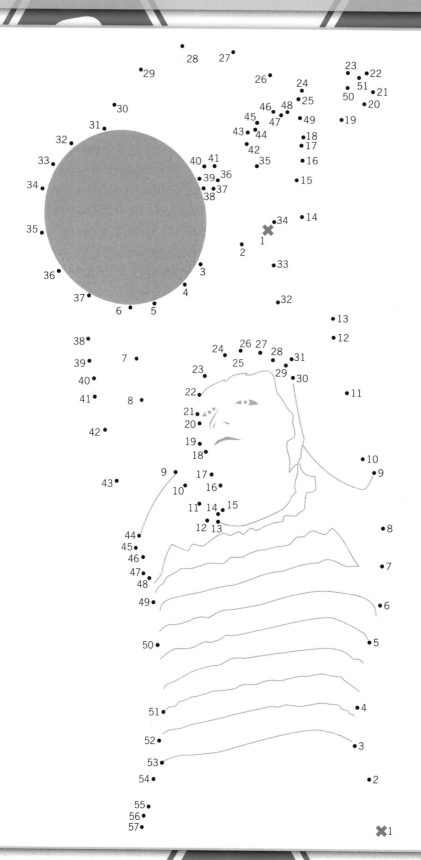

Answers on pages 62/63.

MIX-N-MATCH

See if you can match up the correct stats from last season to the player.

 1. Craig Gordon

 2. Leigh Griffiths

 3. Kieran Tierney

 4. Jack Aitchison

 5. Nir Bitton

 6. Tom Rogic

 7. Stuart Armstrong

 8. Logan Bailly

 9. Scott Brown

 10. Mikael Lustig

10 goals

Five appearances in all competitions

12 European appearances

Three European goals

22 league games and two league goals

One substitute appearance and one goal

40 goals

33 games and one goal

31 games plus eight subs and four goals

Five goals

Answers on pages 62/63.

WORDS OF WISDOM
WHAT THE CELTS WOULD TELL THEIR YOUNGER SELVES

HERE we have Part Two of our Words of Wisdom speeches that your favourite Celts would give to their younger selves.

Part One was on pages 32-33 and here we carry on with the second half. There's plenty of advice for YOU if you fancy a career in the modern game and you could do worse than listen to your heroes in green and white as they tell you just what you have to do to make it with the Hoops.

CRAIG GORDON

I would tell myself that if you want to be a goalkeeper, you have to play as much as you can. Play sport – badminton or squash, anything to help hand-eye coordination and reactions; any sport that could help with that. That definitely helps.

GARY MACKAY-STEVEN

When I was younger I broke my leg in consecutive years and had some other injuries early in my career. My family helped me as there were times when I'd spend long periods on the sidelines. Now I've learned to be positive all the time. Back then it was more my family that helped me through things like injuries. I'd just say to have more of the mindset that I have now which is basically, 'Yes, you'll get obstacles, but if you're positive you'll overcome them'.

KRIS COMMONS

It's got to be to follow your dreams, work hard, take advice on board and enjoy what you do for a living. If you don't, there's no point in doing it.

AIDAN NESBITT

I'm still young but I would say to work hard and listen to what your peers say to you.

EOGHAN O'CONNELL

I'd just say to do everything to the best of your ability. One thing I had when I was younger was the right mentality to deal with a lot of the ups and downs I experienced coming through the Youth Academy. It's important to have that and make sure you enjoy the good times, but don't let the bad times affect you. Keep a level head.

SCOTT BROWN

I would say to enjoy every game. Play every game like it's your last. If you enjoy playing football then it brings the best out in you.

NIR BITTON

The advice I got when I was a kid was that if you have a dream, just do everything possible to get it. Don't listen to other people who try to bring you down. You just have to go and get it for yourself.

IT'S A ROCKIN' ROLE

ENTRY

ENTRY

WE gathered some of the Celts together and asked them which actor they would like to play them if their life was to be featured in a film.

Well, here are their answers and who do you think should play your favourite Celts in a movie of their life?

Scott Allan

Leo DiCaprio. He's the man, isn't he? Every movie he's in, he's brilliant so that's why people pick him. We've obviously got the same barber, too.

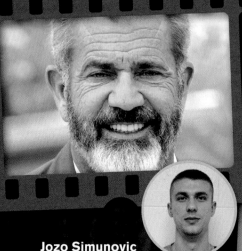

Jozo Simunovic

I'd play myself but I'd have Mel Gibson in the movie somewhere, maybe as my best friend or something.

Ryan Christie

I'll go with Bradley Cooper. He's a really good actor and all the films he's been in have been very good. I thought Limitless was excellent.

Callum McGregor

That's a good question. Ashton Kutcher. I've watched a few of his romcoms but he's also done some serious films too.

Kieran Tierney

Ice Cube would play me well. He has been in a lot of good films, such as Ride Along, 21 Jump Street and Boyz n the Hood.

Saidy Janko

Will Smith or Idris Elba, I like both of them. They are different characters but I just like their acting ability.

Gary Mackay-Steven

It'd need to be someone blond so Ryan Reynolds or DiCaprio. They are two legends, two good looking guys and they're good actors. They wouldn't pick a bad movie either so you could guarantee it'd be good to watch.

Nir Bitton

Wentworth Miller. He plays Michael Scofield in Prison Break. No one ever knows what he's going to do. He's quiet and smart and I really like the way he acts.

Stefan Johansen

Leo DiCaprio. It's a difficult question but I just think he's amazing as an actor. His acting has been so good in all of the movies I've seen with him.

Fiacre Kelleher

Tom Hardy, because I look a bit like him! I'd like to think so anyway. I liked him in Warrior and in the Batman movie, The Dark Knight Rises, as well as The Revenant.

Stuart Armstrong

Who could play me the best? Christoph Waltz. He played the dentist in Django Unchained and he has been in a few other films. He's a really good actor, very versatile, and he would convey on screen what I would want him to.

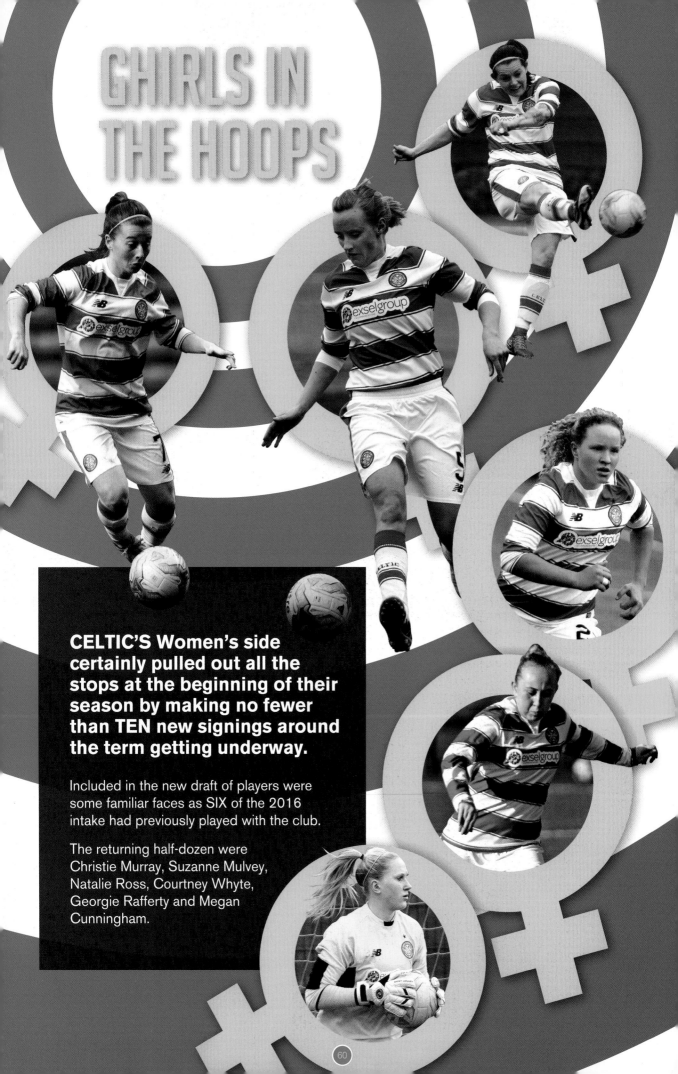

GHIRLS IN THE HOOPS

CELTIC'S Women's side certainly pulled out all the stops at the beginning of their season by making no fewer than TEN new signings around the term getting underway.

Included in the new draft of players were some familiar faces as SIX of the 2016 intake had previously played with the club.

The returning half-dozen were Christie Murray, Suzanne Mulvey, Natalie Ross, Courtney Whyte, Georgie Rafferty and Megan Cunningham.

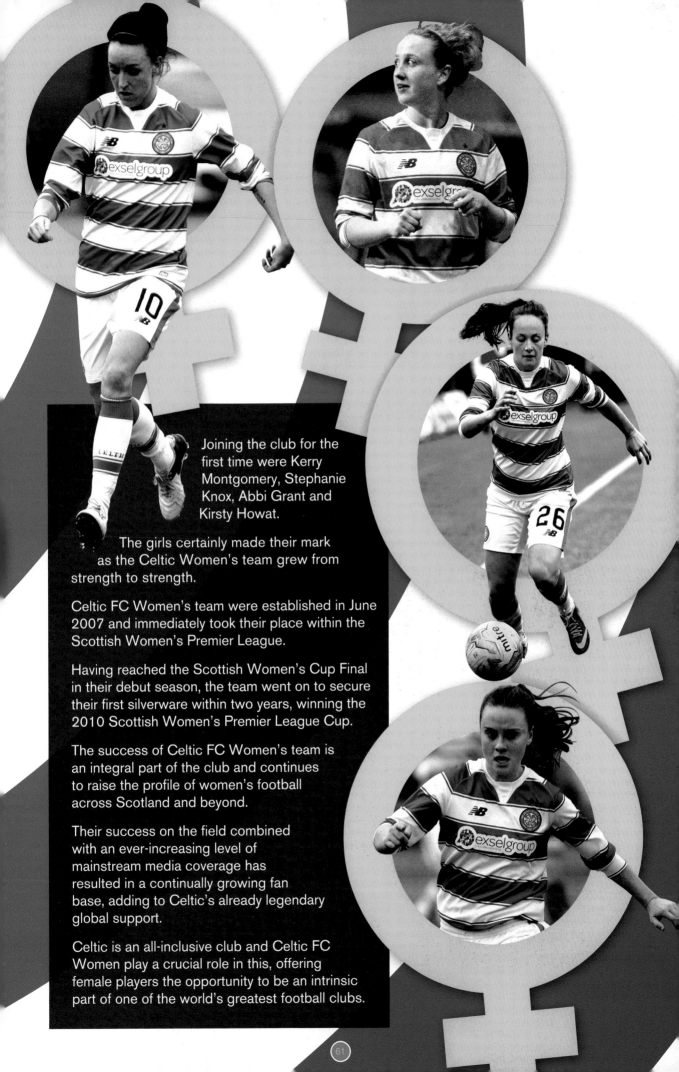

Joining the club for the first time were Kerry Montgomery, Stephanie Knox, Abbi Grant and Kirsty Howat.

The girls certainly made their mark as the Celtic Women's team grew from strength to strength.

Celtic FC Women's team were established in June 2007 and immediately took their place within the Scottish Women's Premier League.

Having reached the Scottish Women's Cup Final in their debut season, the team went on to secure their first silverware within two years, winning the 2010 Scottish Women's Premier League Cup.

The success of Celtic FC Women's team is an integral part of the club and continues to raise the profile of women's football across Scotland and beyond.

Their success on the field combined with an ever-increasing level of mainstream media coverage has resulted in a continually growing fan base, adding to Celtic's already legendary global support.

Celtic is an all-inclusive club and Celtic FC Women play a crucial role in this, offering female players the opportunity to be an intrinsic part of one of the world's greatest football clubs.

QUIZ ANSWERS

PAGE 8 - SPOT THE DIFFERENCE

PAGE 9 - SPFL SEASON 2015/16 QUIZ

1. Ross County
2. Three (Dundee United [A], Hamilton Accies [A] and St Johnstone [A])
3. Dundee United (Durnan) and Inverness Caley Thistle (Devine)
4. Ross County
5. 15
6. Celtic 8-1 Hamilton Accies
7. Dundee (6-0, 0-0 and 0-0)
8. Jack Aitchison
9. Tom Rogic with ten goals
10. Callum McGregor with 12 appearances

PAGE 30 - MAZE

START

FINISH